one-bowl meals

one-bowl meals

SIMPLE, NOURISHING, DELICIOUS

Maria Zizka

Photographs by Erin Scott

ARTISAN | NEW YORK

Library of Congress Cataloging-in-Publication Data

Names: Zizka, Maria, author. | Scott, Erin, photographer.
Title: One-Bowl Meals : Simple, Nourishing, Delicious / by Maria Zizka ;
    photographs by Erin Scott.
Description: New York, NY : Artisan, a division of Workman Publishing
    Co., Inc., [2021] | Includes index.
Identifiers: LCCN 2020042943 | ISBN 9781579659936 (hardcover)
Subjects: LCSH: One-dish meals. | LCGFT: Cookbooks.
Classification: LCC TX693 .Z59 2021 | DDC 641.82—dc23
LC record available at https://lccn.loc.gov/2020042943

Design by Suet Chong

Artisan books are available at special discounts when purchased in
bulk for premiums and sales promotions as well as for fund-raising or
educational use. Special editions or book excerpts also can be created to
specification. For details, contact the Special Sales Director at the address
below, or send an e-mail to specialmarkets@workman.com.

For speaking engagements, contact speakersbureau@workman.com.

Published by Artisan
A division of Workman Publishing Co., Inc.
225 Varick Street
New York, NY 10014-4381
artisanbooks.com

Artisan is a registered trademark of Workman Publishing Co., Inc.

Published simultaneously in Canada by Thomas Allen & Son, Limited

Printed in China

First printing, April 2021

10 9 8 7 6 5 4 3 2 1

for graham

CONTENTS

breakfast

rice

47
Spicy Squash with Rice Cracker Crunch
steamed white rice base + gochujang squash rings + mizuna + seven-minute eggs + rice cracker crunch

49
Tofu-Katsu
steamed white rice base + panko-crusted baked tofu + gingery bok choy + katsu sauce

52
Fried Leftover Rice with Kimchi
kimchi fried rice base + sunny-side-up egg + green onions + radish roots

57
Sushi Set Lunch Special
steamed white rice base + sashimi + wasabi-gomasio cucumber salad + soy sauce + nori

59
Creole Brown Rice
"holy trinity" brown rice base + smoked andouille sausage + sautéed kale

63
Jeweled Rice
spiced basmati rice base + gem-colored dried fruits + toasted pistachios and almonds + roasted chicken

other grains and legumes

69
Very Vert Lentils with Crispy Mustard Chicken
French green lentils base + crispy mustard chicken + spinach + watercress sauce

74
Quinoa with Sheet-Pan Salmon
quinoa base + roasted salmon + caramelized fennel and lemon wheels + lemon-shallot dressing

77
(G)rainbow
barley base + baby spinach + roasted rainbow vegetables + creamy tahini sauce + seven-minute eggs

79
Coconut Farro with Spicy Sole
farro cooked in coconut milk base + spicy sole + chile crisp + cilantro + green onion

83
Tabbouleh, Hold the Greens
bulgur and crispy chickpea base + pomegranate seeds + radish + feta + mint + pomegranate molasses vinaigrette

85
Smoked Salmon on Rye
rye berries base + smoked salmon + creamy dill-juniper sauce

noodles

91
Sesame Soba
soba noodle base + crispy salt-and-pepper tofu + broccolini + black sesame seeds + sesame seed sauce

95
Chicken Paprikash
buttered egg noodle base + saucy chicken + sour cream + parsley

99
Pad Thai
rice noodle base + shrimp + egg + bean sprouts + toasted peanuts + lime + tamarind sauce

101
Sicilian Favorites
ziti pasta base + caponata-style tomato sauce + ricotta salata + toasted pine nuts + parsley

105
Vegan Ramen
ramen noodle base + miso–shiitake mushroom broth + enoki mushrooms + pea shoots + watermelon radish + shichimi togarashi + nori

107
Pasta e Piselli
pappardelle pasta and green peas base + pea shoot salad + crispy pancetta crumbs + Parmigiano

greens

113
Not-Leafy Caesar
thinly sliced fennel base + anchovy croutons + seven-minute eggs + garlicky dressing

117
Scandinavian Salad
arugula base + tarragon cream sauce + smoked trout + pickled pink onions

119
Salade Niçoise
chicories base + haricots verts + tuna + Niçoise olives + new potatoes + Dijon vinaigrette

124
Antipasto
romaine lettuce base + cured meats + cheese + pickled vegetables + Italian-style dressing

127
Panzanella Caprese
mixed baby greens base + tomatoes + torn croutons + mozzarella + basil

129
Shrimp Taco Salad
green cabbage base + tomato rice + chipotle shrimp + tortilla chips + crispy pepitas + avocado + lime

INTRODUCTION

In recent years, the one-bowl meal has become a staple of contemporary eating, but the idea of a complete meal in a bowl is not new: think of Korean bibimbap, a sizzling hot stone bowl of rice served with a colorful array of pickles, spicy chile sauce, and an egg; or traditional Japanese donburi rice bowls topped with vegetables and meat or seafood; porridge with flavorful toppings is a classic bowl both in the United Kingdom and across Southeast Asia. In many cuisines, the nutritional power couple of beans and rice unite in one bowl. Whether it's savory or sweet, Mediterranean or Scandinavian, a bowl offers a nourishing, personalized, and delicious meal in one.

But what exactly is a bowl? Let's go with an easy answer! In this book, a bowl is defined by the following equation:

bowl = base + topping + topping + sauce (sometimes)

Are you wondering about that sometimes? We'll get there, but first let's start with the foundation of every good bowl—the base. The chapters in this book are organized around their base ingredient: rice, other grains and legumes, noodles, or greens. (The Breakfast chapter has recipes with a variety of bases, including yogurt, oatmeal, and eggs.) Greens can be rinsed, dried, and stored in the refrigerator until you're ready to use them. Noodles are generally best cooked the day you eat them, but rice and other grain bases can be cooked ahead, and you might even consider making a double or triple batch for a week of meals. Most of these recipes make two generous servings, and they all scale easily. Yield is a little tricky to determine with a one-bowl meal. The amount that you'd like to eat varies from day to day, not to mention from person to person. These recipes err on the side of having plenty of base ingredient in each bowl. That way, you're sure to cook enough to fill you up on your hungriest day, and if you prefer to save some for leftovers, then that's great, too.

A bowl needs at least a couple of toppings. However, quality is much more important than quantity—two delicious toppings are better than four that are just so-so. The best bowls have a variety of flavors, textures, and colors.

Protein plays a valuable role, contributing nutritious and filling qualities. Most recipes in this book include a protein, and all the recipes can be adapted to suit your tastes. In some cases, the base is a protein (like in Very Vert Lentils, page 69). Or one of the toppings could be a protein (like in Shrimp Taco Salad, page 129). Feel free to improvise by including protein in the form of dairy, eggs, tofu, beans, meat, or seafood. If you're looking to eat vegetarian, vegan, or gluten-free, you'll find plenty of options and endless variations on the recipes.

Eggs are super-quick-cooking and affordable sources of protein. When you top a bowl with a soft-boiled egg, the runny yolk acts like a built-in sauce, cloaking the other ingredients with its rich flavor. Here's a foolproof recipe to turn to anytime you want to put an egg on it:

Seven-Minute Eggs

2 large eggs (or as many as you like)

Bring a small pot of water to a boil. (Use a medium saucepan for 6 or more eggs.) Carefully lower in the eggs, adjust the heat so that the water simmers gently, and cook for exactly 7 minutes. (If you're starting with fridge-cold eggs, after 7 minutes of cooking, the whites will be set and the yolks will be soft and a little runny in the centers; if you prefer egg yolks that are fully set, cook the eggs for 10 minutes total.) Transfer the cooked eggs to a bowl of ice water and let cool for 2 minutes, then crack and peel away the shells.

For tinned seafood like anchovies and tuna, make sure to choose sustainably caught fish packed in 100 percent extra-virgin olive oil. Buy cheese and smoked fish from local shops, if you can, or order online. (Check out Sources, page 135.)

Now, about that sometimes-sauce idea. Not every bowl benefits from a sauce, because sometimes there's already a creamy component working its magic, such as yogurt, cheese, or the aforementioned runny egg yolk. Remember that putting together a balanced bowl means exercising restraint and respecting the inherent qualities of the ingredients.

Last, the bowls in this book are often garnished with a crunchy or bright element. A finishing touch like toasted nuts or seeds looks beautiful and adds a little surprise. Pickled Pink Onions (page 117) lend their tart pop to all kinds of bowls, from Chilaquiles Rojos (page 37) to Smoked Salmon on Rye (page 85). Sometimes the simplest flourish of a few fresh herb leaves is all you need. Toasting nuts at home doesn't

take too much time and really amps up their flavor. Here's how to do it like a pro:

How to Toast Nuts in an Oven

Spread out the nuts on a baking sheet and toast in a 300°F (150°C) oven, stirring every 4 minutes or so, until golden brown inside. (Cut one in half to check.) Immediately transfer the nuts to a plate so that they don't continue to cook on the hot baking sheet and burn. Let cool completely before transferring to an airtight container. Toasted nuts keep well for 2 to 3 weeks at room temperature.

	walnut halves	pistachios	whole almonds	shelled peanuts	pine nuts
time in oven	5 to 8 minutes	6 to 8 minutes	16 to 18 minutes	15 to 20 minutes	6 to 9 minutes

If you're toasting three tablespoons or fewer of nuts or seeds, follow the quicker stovetop method on page 64.

A word on substitutions: Some people will tell you that you can mix and match bowl components willy-nilly. This just isn't true. Or, at least, you won't always end up with a winning combination of flavors. While the bowl is indeed a flexible template, there are certain ingredients that play well (or not) with others. Your goal is for everything in the bowl to go together perfectly. For example, in the Tofu-Katsu bowl (page 49), the panko-crusted tofu has a distinct character, but it also partners seamlessly with the steamed white rice base and the gingery bok choy. If you keep the following guidelines in mind, you'll have no trouble customizing tasty bowls.

substitution rules of thumb

For all the recipes in the Rice chapter, you can opt for white or brown rice. Just make sure to use the same size—short- or long-grain—as specified in the recipe.

    If you're wondering about swapping one alternative grain or legume for another, consult this chart:

	Barley (cooked according to the recipe on page 77)	Lentils (cooked according to the recipe on page 69)	Quinoa (cooked according to the recipe on page 74)	Farro (cooked according to the recipe on page 79)	Chickpeas & Bulgur (cooked according to the recipe on page 83)	Rye Berries (cooked according to the recipe on page 85)
G(rainbow)		✗	✓	✓ *cook like barley	✓	✓
Very Vert Lentils with Crispy Mustard Chicken	✓		✓	✓ *cook like barley	✓	✓
Quinoa with Sheet-Pan Salmon	✓	✓		✓ *cook like barley	✓	✓
Coconut Farro with Spicy Sole	✓ *cook like farro	✗	✓		✗	✓ *cook like farro
Tabbouleh, Hold the Greens	✓	✗	✓	✓ *cook like barley		✓
Smoked Salmon on Rye	✓	✗	✗	✓ *cook like barley	✗	

*   When substituting grains, always cook the grain according to the instructions in its original recipe, except where noted.

When a recipe calls for a fresh, tender herb (such as parsley, basil, dill, mint, or chervil), feel free to use just about any fresh, tender herb that you love. The exception is cilantro, which tends to work best in recipes that also have soy sauce and/or something spicy (like chile pepper) as an ingredient. For Panzanella Caprese (page 127), you should probably stick to basil because tomato, mozzarella, and basil form an iconic combo.

No fancy equipment or tools are required in this book. If you happen to have a rice cooker, of course you can use it to make rice. But if you don't, rest assured that all these recipes have been developed and thoroughly tested on a stovetop.

There's something comforting and cozy about eating a personalized meal in a bowl. Putting together the base and the toppings is a satisfyingly creative act, one that's ideal for busy home cooks because most components can be prepared in advance. When you're ready to eat, just assemble and serve. Simple, nourishing, delicious.

how to bowl in 5 steps

1. start with a base
check out the different
chapters in this book

2. include a protein
dairy, eggs, tofu, beans,
meat, or seafood

3. consider a sauce

especially if there's not
already a creamy element

4. add a couple of toppings

create a variety of
textures and colors
in the bowl

5. garnish

with something crunchy
or bright—like toasted nuts
or seeds or fresh herbs

breakfast

yogurt, fruit, and granola

yogurt base	+	broiled pineapple	+	honey-lime syrup	+	gluten-free granola

Serves 2 • This sunny yogurt bowl is topped with pumpkin seed–studded granola. You'll have plenty of granola left over. It keeps well for weeks and is delicious on its own. For the pineapple, you can, of course, use a whole fresh fruit cut into ½-inch (1 cm) slices, but the canned slices are so quick and they taste great—just make sure to choose the kind in 100 percent juice, not syrup.

TOPPINGS

GLUTEN-FREE GRANOLA

4 cups (400 g) old-fashioned rolled oats

½ cup (45 g) sliced almonds

½ cup (60 g) hulled pumpkin seeds (aka pepitas)

½ teaspoon fine sea salt

½ cup (1 stick/115 g) unsalted butter

½ cup (120 ml) honey

BROILED PINEAPPLE

1 (8-ounce/225 g) can of pineapple slices in 100% pineapple juice

SYRUP

1½ tablespoons honey

1½ tablespoons fresh lime juice

BASE

2 cups (500 g) whole-milk plain yogurt

Make the granola topping: Heat the oven to 300°F (150°C). Line a rimmed baking sheet with parchment paper.

In a large bowl, stir together the oats, almonds, pumpkin seeds, and salt. In a small saucepan, melt the butter and then stir in the honey. Pour the honey-butter over the oat mixture and stir until incorporated. Spread out the oat mixture on the prepared baking sheet. Bake for 15 minutes, stir, then bake until golden brown, another 15 minutes. Let cool. Granola can be made ahead and stored in an airtight container at room temperature for up to 2 weeks.

Make the syrup: Stir together the honey and lime juice until completely blended.

To prepare the pineapple, heat the broiler to high. Arrange the pineapple in a single layer on a baking sheet. Place under the broiler, rotating the baking sheet as needed to promote even browning, until dark brown in a few places, 5 to 10 minutes. Keep a close eye on the fruit—it can brown quickly or slowly, depending on the strength of your broiler.

Divide the yogurt between 2 bowls. Top with the broiled pineapple, a drizzle of honey-lime syrup, and some granola.

yogurt, fruit, and granola, see page 24

vegan chia seed pudding with tropical fruit salad

chia seed pudding base	+	tropical fruit	+	toasted coconut flakes

Serves 2 • Cashew milk has a luxuriously creamy texture that is perfect for this vegan pudding, although any dairy-free milk will do. You can use other tropical fruits like papaya and passion fruit—just keep the overall quantity of fruit approximately the same.

BASE

2 cups (480 ml) sweetened cashew milk (or your favorite dairy-free milk)

½ cup (80 g) chia seeds

¼ teaspoon pure vanilla extract

1 orange

TOPPINGS

TROPICAL FRUIT SALAD

1 banana, sliced

¾ cup (about 4 ounces/115 g) chopped mango

1 kiwi, sliced

1 tablespoon brown or granulated sugar

⅓ cup (30 g) sweetened or unsweetened coconut flakes

The night before, make the pudding: In a medium bowl, stir together the cashew milk, chia seeds, vanilla, and 1 teaspoon finely grated zest from the orange (keep the zested orange for the fruit salad). Stir continuously for 20 to 30 seconds to disperse the chia seeds. Let the mixture rest for about 5 minutes, then stir continuously for another 20 to 30 seconds. This will help to evenly distribute the seeds and prevent them from clumping together. Pour the mixture into 2 small bowls. Cover and refrigerate until thickened, at least 2 hours (or overnight).

Make the fruit salad: In a medium bowl, combine the banana, mango, kiwi, and sugar. Using an extremely sharp knife, cut off the top and bottom of the reserved zested orange. Set the orange on one cut side so that it doesn't roll around. Place the blade of your knife at the top of the orange and cut down, tracing the curved line of the fruit, to remove a section of the peel and white pith. Rotate the orange and continue cutting away the peel and pith until you've removed it all. Go back and trim any pith still clinging to the fruit. Slice the orange crosswise into thin rounds, discarding any seeds, and add the rounds to the bowl of other fruits. Stir gently to mix.

In a dry skillet, toast the coconut flakes over medium heat, stirring often, until golden brown, about 3 minutes.

To serve, spoon the tropical fruit salad into the bowls of pudding. Scatter the toasted coconut on top of the fruit.

oatmeal with apple pie toppings

toasted steel-cut oats base	+	sugared apples	+	crème fraîche	+	lemon zest

Serves 2 • For everyone who wakes up with a sweet tooth, this oatmeal bowl is a little like dessert for breakfast. In addition to tasting great, the toasted steel-cut oats base will keep you full for hours and give you the energy you need to start the day.

BASE

4 cups (960 ml) water

2 cups (480 ml) almond milk or water

1 tablespoon unsalted butter

1½ cups (300 g) steel-cut oats

Fine sea salt

TOPPINGS

SUGARED APPLES

2 tablespoons light or dark brown sugar

½ teaspoon ground cinnamon

1 apple, cored and thinly sliced

¼ cup (60 g) crème fraîche or plain whole-milk yogurt

Finely grated lemon zest

In a medium saucepan, bring the water and almond milk to a simmer (alternatively, you can skip the almond milk and use a total of 6 cups [1.5 liters] of water). While it heats up, melt the butter in a large skillet over medium heat. Add the oats and a big pinch of salt to the butter and cook, stirring often, until fragrant and toasted, about 3 minutes. Stir the toasted oats into the milk mixture. Cook over medium-low heat, stirring occasionally and then more frequently as the oats get closer to being done, until very thick and creamy, 25 to 30 minutes.

Meanwhile, in a medium bowl, combine the brown sugar and cinnamon and mix well. Add the sliced apple and toss to coat.

When the oats are done, divide them between 2 bowls and top each with half of the apple mixture, a dollop of crème fraîche, and a pinch of lemon zest.

savory porridge

| toasted steel-cut oats base | + | frizzled shallots | + | soft-cooked eggs | + | herbs |

Serves 2 ▪ Oatmeal doesn't always have to be sweet. It can lean deliciously to the savory side when you top it with soft-cooked eggs, fresh herbs, and crispy frizzled shallots, which are much easier to make than you might be imagining. They're also wonderful sprinkled over rice bowls, Sesame Soba (page 91), and Pad Thai (page 99).

BASE

6 cups (1.5 liters) chicken broth or water

1 tablespoon unsalted butter

1½ cups (300 g) steel-cut oats

Fine sea salt

Freshly ground black pepper

TOPPINGS

FRIZZLED SHALLOTS

1 large or 2 small shallots, peeled and very thinly sliced

½ cup (120 ml) vegetable oil

2 Seven-Minute Eggs (see page 14), peeled and halved

¼ cup (5 g) fresh tender herb leaves (such as cilantro, chervil, or flat-leaf parsley)

Make the porridge: In a medium saucepan, bring the broth to a simmer. While it heats up, melt the butter in a large skillet over medium heat. Add the oats to the butter and cook, stirring often, until fragrant and toasted, about 3 minutes. Stir the toasted oats into the broth. Cook, uncovered, over medium-low heat, stirring occasionally and then more frequently as the oats get closer to being done, until very thick and creamy, 25 to 30 minutes. When the oats are done, taste them and season with salt and pepper.

While the oats cook, make the frizzled shallots. Line a plate with paper towels or a clean brown paper bag and set aside. Place the shallots in a small saucepan and pour in the vegetable oil. Cook over medium-low heat, stirring occasionally, until the shallots are mostly brown, 10 to 18 minutes. Keep a close eye on the shallots once they are golden. They can go from brown to burned pretty quickly! Strain the fried shallots through a fine-mesh sieve and then spread them out on the prepared plate. (Save the flavorful shallot oil for another recipe; try substituting it for the olive oil in Coconut Farro with Spicy Sole, page 79.)

Divide the oats between 2 bowls and top each with frizzled shallots, a soft-cooked egg, and fresh herbs.

chilaquiles rojos

tortilla chips base + ancho chile sauce + soft-scrambled eggs + pinto beans + avocado + cotija

Serves 2 • Chilaquiles is a quick, satisfying breakfast, and it makes for an easy weeknight dinner as well. The tortilla chips base, ancho chile sauce, and eggs are nonnegotiable, but the other toppings are up to you. Add fresh cilantro if you love it; omit it if you don't.

ANCHO CHILE SAUCE

2 dried ancho chiles

1 plum tomato

1 garlic clove

¼ teaspoon fine sea salt

TOPPINGS

SOFT-SCRAMBLED EGGS

1 tablespoon unsalted butter

2 large eggs

Fine sea salt

Freshly ground black pepper

½ (15-ounce/425 g) can of pinto beans, drained and rinsed

½ avocado, sliced

¼ cup (5 g) fresh cilantro leaves (optional)

3 tablespoons crumbled cotija cheese

BASE

4 cups (100 g) thick-cut tortilla chips

Make the sauce: Bring a kettle or a small pot filled with water to a boil. Meanwhile, tear each chile in half, discard the stem and seeds, and drop the torn chiles into a large, dry skillet. Toast over medium-high heat, turning the chiles often, until fragrant and softened, about 2 minutes. Transfer the chiles to a medium bowl and pour in enough boiling water to cover. Let soak for 15 minutes. (No need to wash the skillet; you'll use it again for the chile sauce.) Use tongs to transfer the chiles to a blender and add the tomato, garlic, salt, and ¾ cup (180 ml) of the chile soaking water. Blend until smooth.

Pour the ancho chile sauce into the skillet and bring to a simmer.

While the sauce is cooking, prepare the toppings: In a small pan, melt the butter over medium-low heat. In a small bowl, whisk the eggs just until the yolks and whites are combined, add them to the pan, and cook, stirring often with a fork, until scrambled and set. Season with salt and pepper.

In a separate small pan, warm the beans with a splash of water over medium-low heat. Slice the avocado and make sure the cilantro (if using) and cotija are ready to go.

Just before you are ready to serve, add the tortilla chips to the pan of sauce. Stir to coat. Divide the sauced chips between 2 serving bowls. Top with the soft-scrambled eggs, warm beans, avocado, cilantro, and cotija.

four-pepper shakshuka, see page 42

four-pepper shakshuka

| spiced tomato cream and baked eggs base | + | za'atar-sumac drizzle | + | feta | + | warm pita bread |

Serves 2 · There are four different kinds of peppers in this shakshuka: fresh red bell pepper, paprika, chile flakes, and black pepper. There's also a spoonful of cream in the tomato sauce, which is definitely not traditional but does balance the heat from the peppers with a little richness.

BASE

2 tablespoons extra-virgin olive oil

½ small yellow or red onion, finely chopped

½ red bell pepper, finely chopped

Fine sea salt

1 tablespoon tomato paste

½ teaspoon smoked paprika (sweet or hot)

Pinch of chile flakes

1 (15-ounce/425 g) can of diced tomatoes

2 tablespoons heavy cream

3 or 4 large eggs

Freshly ground black pepper

ZA'ATAR-SUMAC DRIZZLE

1 tablespoon za'atar

2 teaspoons sumac

2 tablespoons extra-virgin olive oil

TOPPINGS

2 or 3 pita breads

4 ounces (115 g) feta, crumbled

Heat the oven to 375°F (190°C).

In a medium oven-safe skillet, warm the olive oil over medium heat. Add the onion, bell pepper, and ¼ teaspoon of salt. Cook, stirring often, until softened, about 5 minutes. Stir in the tomato paste, paprika, and chile flakes and cook for 1 minute. Add the diced tomatoes, cream, and ½ teaspoon of salt. Bring to a simmer and cook for 3 to 4 minutes. Remove the skillet from the heat, use the back of a spoon to create 3 or 4 wells in the tomato-cream mixture, and crack 1 egg into each well. Season the eggs with salt and pepper. Carefully transfer the skillet to the oven and bake until the egg whites are just set but the yolks are still runny (try shaking the pan to see if the yolks jiggle), 6 to 10 minutes. Place the pita breads directly on the oven rack for the last few minutes of cooking time to warm them. They only need about 3 minutes—any longer and they start turning into crisp pita chips.

Meanwhile, make the drizzle: In a small bowl, stir together the za'atar, sumac, and oil.

Serve the eggs and spiced tomato cream in the skillet family-style, or transfer to 2 individual bowls. Drizzle the za'atar-sumac oil over the shakshuka, scatter the feta on top, and serve with warm pitas to mop up all the delicious sauce.

rice

U.S.#1 EXTRA FANCY

THE UNIQUE

NEW VARIETY

California's Original

SUSHI RICE

spicy squash with rice cracker crunch

steamed white rice base	+	gochujang squash rings	+	mizuna	+	seven-minute eggs	+	rice cracker crunch

Serves 2 · You can find many kinds of rice crackers at Asian grocery stores. While you're there, look for peppery mizuna leaves (also known as Japanese mustard greens); they have beautiful frilly edges. If you can't find them, try arugula or watercress. Of all the hard-skinned winter squashes, delicata and acorn are perhaps the easiest to cook because you don't need to peel them.

TOPPINGS

GOCHUJANG SQUASH RINGS

1 tablespoon gochujang

1 tablespoon soy sauce or tamari

2 tablespoons vegetable oil

1 small (about 1¼ pounds/565 g) delicata or acorn squash, sliced crosswise into ½-inch (1 cm) rings or half-moons, ends and seeds discarded

4 large green onions, white and green parts, cut into 3-inch (7.5 cm) segments

3 tablespoons rice crackers

1 handful of mizuna leaves (see headnote)

2 Seven-Minute Eggs (page 14), peeled and cut in half

BASE

3 cups (720 ml) water

1½ cups (300 g) short-grain white rice, rinsed

¾ teaspoon fine sea salt

Heat the oven to 425°F (220°C).

In a large bowl, stir together the gochujang, soy sauce, and vegetable oil. Add the squash rings and green onions and toss to coat. Spread out the squash and green onions on a rimmed baking sheet, drizzling any leftover marinade from the bowl over them. Roast until tender and browned around the edges, 20 to 25 minutes. Flip them after about 10 minutes for even browning on both sides.

Meanwhile, in a medium saucepan, bring the water to a boil. Add the rice and salt. Decrease the heat to medium-low, cover the pot, and cook for 18 minutes, until all the water has been absorbed. Remove the lid, fluff the rice with a fork, then return the lid and allow the rice to rest off the heat for 10 minutes before serving.

Place the rice crackers in a ziptop bag and use a rolling pin to smash them into large crumbs.

Divide the steamed rice between 2 bowls. Scatter the mizuna leaves over the rice and then top with the roasted squash rings and green onions. Nestle an egg into each bowl. Sprinkle the rice cracker crunch over everything.

tofu-katsu

| steamed white rice base | + | panko-crusted baked tofu | + | gingery bok choy | + | katsu sauce |

Serves 2 · The panko-crusted tofu that tops this rice bowl has a crispy exterior and a meltingly soft interior. It looks like it has been fried, but it's actually baked in the oven! For store-bought katsu sauce, see if you can find Bachan's, a fantastic teriyaki-ish Japanese-style barbecue sauce. You can also mix your own katsu sauce by stirring together ¼ cup (70 g) ketchup, 2 tablespoons Worcestershire sauce, 2 teaspoons soy sauce or tamari, and a pinch of sugar.

BASE

3 cups (600 g) steamed short-grain white rice (see page 47)

TOPPINGS

PANKO-CRUSTED BAKED TOFU

7 or 8 ounces (200 or 225 g) firm tofu

¼ cup (30 g) all-purpose flour

1 large egg

½ cup (30 g) panko breadcrumbs

½ teaspoon fine sea salt

Freshly ground black pepper

GINGERY BOK CHOY

1 tablespoon sesame oil

1 garlic clove, sliced

1-inch (2.5 cm) piece of ginger, peeled and cut into matchsticks

4 to 6 baby bok choy (about 6 ounces/170 g total), halved lengthwise

2 tablespoons water

1 tablespoon soy sauce or tamari

1 green onion, white and green parts, thinly sliced

Katsu sauce, for serving

Heat the oven to 400°F (200°C). Line a baking sheet with parchment paper.

Pat the tofu dry with paper towels and cut into 6 equal pieces. On a large plate, spread out the flour. In a shallow bowl, beat the egg. On another large plate, stir together the panko, salt, and several grinds of pepper. Coat each tofu piece on all sides with the flour, then dunk it in the egg, and then dredge it in the panko mixture, pressing to adhere the crumbs to all sides of the tofu. Place the coated tofu pieces on the prepared baking sheet. Bake for 15 minutes, then flip and bake until golden brown and crisp, about 20 minutes more.

When the tofu is almost done baking, make the gingery bok choy: In a large skillet with a lid, heat the sesame oil over medium heat. Add the garlic and ginger and cook, stirring constantly, for 1 minute. Add the bok choy, water, and soy sauce. Cover the pan and cook for 3 minutes, until the bok choy is just tender.

To assemble the bowls, make beds of steamed rice in 2 bowls and add the gingery bok choy and baked tofu to each. Scatter the green onion on top and serve the katsu sauce on the side.

fried leftover rice with kimchi

kimchi fried rice base	+	sunny-side-up egg	+	green onions	+	radish roots

Serves 2 • Leftover rice is the secret ingredient to the best fried rice. It's already a little dried out, so it crisps nicely in the pan. If you are starting from scratch, though, you can follow the rice-cooking instructions on page 48 for white rice or page 60 for brown rice, then spread out the cooked rice on a baking sheet and let it cool completely before frying.

BASE

3 tablespoons vegetable oil

2 garlic cloves, thinly sliced

2 green onions, white and green parts, thinly sliced

3 cups (600 g) cooked and cooled short-grain white or brown rice

½ cup (75 g) drained and chopped kimchi

1 tablespoon soy sauce or tamari

TOPPINGS

SUNNY-SIDE-UP EGGS

1 tablespoon vegetable oil

2 large eggs

Fine sea salt

Freshly ground black pepper

1 handful of radish shoots (about 1 ounce/30 g; optional)

1 green onion, white and green parts, thinly sliced

Heat a large nonstick skillet over medium-high heat for 1 minute. Pour in 1 tablespoon of the vegetable oil and add the garlic and green onions. Cook, stirring constantly, for 1 minute. Transfer the garlic and onions to a small plate. Pour in the remaining 2 tablespoons oil, swirling the pan to coat the entire surface. Add the rice, stir briefly to coat it in the oil, then spread it out in an even layer. Let cook, without stirring, until the rice crisps, 2 to 3 minutes. Stir the rice, spread it out again in an even layer, and cook, without stirring, for another 3 minutes.

Return the cooked garlic and green onions to the skillet along with the kimchi and soy sauce. Stir well and cook, without stirring once again, for about another 3 minutes, until there are some crispy browned rice grains. If the rice isn't browned yet, repeat the process of stirring and then cooking without stirring for about 3 minutes.

Divide the fried rice between 2 bowls and return the skillet to medium-high heat. Drizzle in the vegetable oil, swirling the pan to coat the entire surface, then crack in the eggs and season them with a pinch each of salt and pepper. Cook until the whites are set but the yolks are still runny, 2 to 4 minutes.

Top each bowl of fried rice with a sunny-side-up egg, some radish shoots (if using), and a sprinkling of green onion.

leftover fried rice with kimchi, see page 52

sushi set lunch special

| steamed white rice base | + | sashimi | + | wasabi-gomasio cucumber salad | + | soy sauce | + | nori |

Serves 2 • For this bowl, choose the freshest and highest-quality fish you can find; salmon, yellowtail, and tuna all work well. Gomasio is a Japanese seasoning blend traditionally made from coarsely ground sesame seeds and salt. You can use plain toasted sesame seeds instead, but then make sure to add a little salt to the cucumber salad.

BASE

3 cups (600 g) steamed short-grain white rice (see page 47)

TOPPINGS

WASABI-GOMASIO CUCUMBER SALAD

1 tablespoon mayonnaise (or use wasabi mayonnaise and skip the wasabi powder)

¾ teaspoon wasabi powder or prepared wasabi

1 tablespoon rice vinegar

1 teaspoon sugar

1 teaspoon sesame oil

2 Persian or 1 small English cucumber, thinly sliced

Fine sea salt (optional)

2 tablespoons gomasio or toasted sesame seeds (see headnote)

4 to 5 ounces (115 to 140 g) sashimi-grade raw fish (such as salmon, yellowtail, or tuna)

2 shiso leaves (optional)

2 sheets of nori, cut into 2-inch (5 cm) strips

Soy sauce or tamari, for serving

First, make the cucumber salad: In a medium bowl, combine the mayonnaise, wasabi, vinegar, sugar, and sesame oil. Add the cucumber, mix well, and taste, adding a little salt if needed. You can also add more wasabi if you want the salad to be spicier. Sprinkle the gomasio on top.

Place the fish on a clean cutting board. Using a very sharp knife, cut the fish into thin slices. I like them to be somewhere between ½ inch (1 cm) and ¼ inch (6 mm) thick. Try to cut each slice in one decisive movement, avoiding any back-and-forth sawing gestures. If the fish feels too soft, you can freeze it to firm it up, checking its firmness after 15 minutes or so. Once the fish has been sliced, it tastes best served right away.

To assemble the bowls, divide the steamed rice between 2 bowls. Arrange the cucumber salad in a little pile on one side of each bowl. Fan out the sashimi slices on the other side. Tuck the shiso, if using, and the nori strips into the side of each bowl and serve with a small dish of soy sauce (or tamari) for dipping.

creole brown rice

| "holy trinity" brown rice base | + | smoked andouille sausage | + | sautéed kale |

Serves 2 • In Cajun and Louisiana Creole cuisines, "the holy trinity" refers to yellow onion, celery, and green bell pepper, three aromatic vegetables that, when combined, give layers of flavor to dishes like this brown rice bowl. You can top the bowl with any kind of sausage you like, but smoked andouille pairs especially nicely.

BASE

1½ cups (300 g) long-grain brown rice

Fine sea salt

¼ cup (60 ml) extra-virgin olive oil

1 small or ½ large yellow onion, finely chopped

2 celery stalks, finely chopped

1 green bell pepper, seeded and finely chopped

1 teaspoon smoked paprika (sweet or hot)

1 teaspoon dried oregano

Pinch of cayenne

¼ teaspoon freshly ground black pepper

TOPPINGS

1 tablespoon extra-virgin olive oil

1 or 2 smoked andouille sausages, sliced lengthwise and then crosswise into ½-inch (1 cm) half-moons

4 ounces (115 g) kale, stemmed and coarsely chopped (about 4 cups)

Fine sea salt

Freshly ground black pepper

The night before you'd like to eat this bowl, soak the rice in plenty of cool water with a pinch of salt for about 10 hours, or overnight. The next day, bring a medium pot of salted water to a boil. Drain the rice, add it to the boiling water, and cook until tender but not mushy, 20 to 40 minutes. Drain. Cooked brown rice keeps well, covered, in the fridge for 3 days.

Cook the toppings: Heat a large skillet over medium-high heat. Swirl the 1 tablespoon of olive oil in the pan and add the sliced sausage. Cook, without stirring, until browned on the first side, about 2 minutes. Flip and cook on the second side until browned, 1 to 2 minutes more. Transfer the sausage to a plate. Add the kale to the pan. Season with salt and pepper and cook, stirring occasionally, until wilted and vibrantly green, 2 to 3 minutes. Transfer the kale to the plate with the sausage. Keep warm in a 250°F (120°C) oven until you're ready to assemble the bowls.

To finish the rice, using the same skillet as used for the sausage and kale, set the skillet over medium heat. Swirl in the ¼ cup (60 ml) of olive oil. Add the onion, celery, bell pepper, paprika, oregano, cayenne, black pepper, and 1 teaspoon of salt. Cook, stirring occasionally, until softened, about 5 minutes. Add the boiled rice to the pan of cooked vegetables. Return the pan to medium heat. Stir well to mix the rice and vegetables and cook until everything is hot.

To serve, divide the rice between 2 bowls. Top with the sausage and kale.

jeweled rice

spiced basmati rice base   +   gem-colored dried fruits   +   toasted pistachios and almonds   +   roasted chicken

Serves 2 • A gorgeous array of toppings makes this rice bowl one of the prettiest in the chapter. Soaking the gem-colored dried fruits in hot water allows them to plump up and taste as good as they look.

BASE

¼ cup (½ stick/55 g) unsalted butter

2 tablespoons extra-virgin olive oil

2 garlic cloves, sliced

3 green onions, white and light green parts thinly sliced, dark green tops thinly sliced and reserved for garnish

1½ cups (300 g) basmati or other long-grain white rice, rinsed

½ teaspoon ground turmeric

3 cardamom pods

1 cinnamon stick

½ teaspoon fine sea salt

Freshly ground black pepper

2½ cups (600 ml) water

TOPPINGS

6 dried apricots, cut lengthwise into halves (or quarters if large)

2 tablespoons dried sour cherries

2 tablespoons golden raisins

2 tablespoons pistachios

2 tablespoons slivered almonds

¾ cup (about 4 ounces/115 g) shredded homemade or store-bought roasted chicken (not pictured)

Flaky sea salt

In a heavy-bottomed medium saucepan with a lid, warm the butter and olive oil over medium heat. When the butter has melted, add the garlic and the white and light green parts of the onions, and cook, stirring constantly, for 1 minute. Add the rice, turmeric, cardamom pods, cinnamon stick, fine salt, and several grinds of pepper. Cook, stirring, until the spices are fragrant, about 3 minutes. Pour in the water. Cover the pot, decrease the heat to medium-low, and cook for 18 minutes, until the rice is tender and has absorbed the water. Remove the lid and pick out and discard the cardamom pods and cinnamon stick. Using a wooden spoon, stir the rice and scrape up any crispy browned bits.

While the rice is cooking, place the dried fruit in individual bowls to keep them separate. Pour enough hot water from the tap into each bowl to cover the fruit. Let soak until each fruit has plumped up, about 5 minutes. Drain the soaked fruit and squeeze them to remove any excess water.

In a small, dry skillet over medium heat, toast the nuts, one type at a time to keep them separate, until fragrant and golden, 2 to 5 minutes.

To serve, divide the rice between 2 bowls. Arrange each topping—the dried fruits, the toasted nuts, and the dark green parts of the onions—in distinct rows or scatter them all. Top with the roasted chicken and garnish with a pinch of flaky salt.

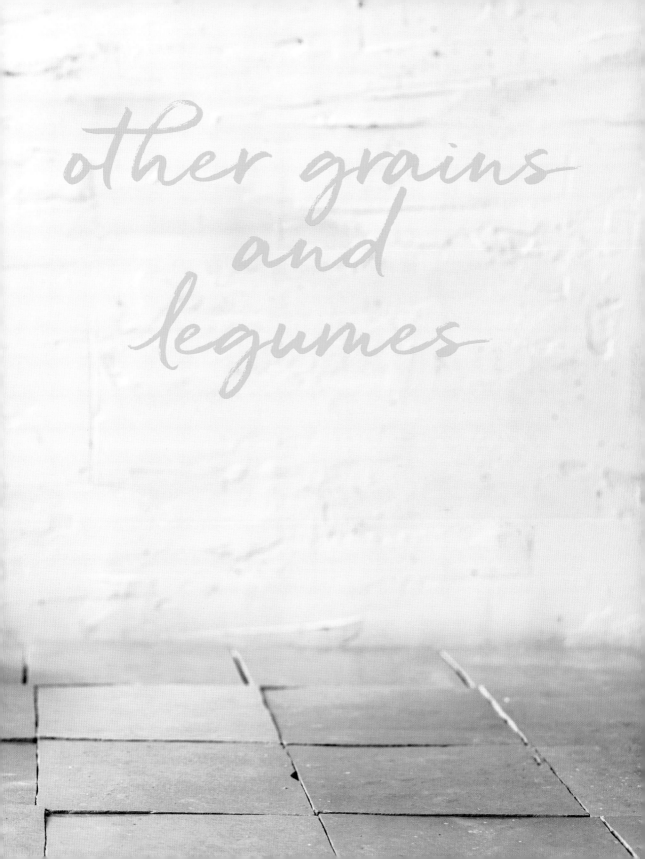

other grains
and
legumes

very vert lentils with crispy mustard chicken

French green lentils base + crispy mustard chicken + spinach + watercress sauce

Serves 2 ▪ In this very green bowl, little French green lentils (sometimes called lentilles du Puy) are topped with leafy spinach and a vibrant sauce made from watercress. Crispy mustard chicken turns it into a meal. For a vegetarian alternative, swap out the chicken for Seven-Minute Eggs (page 14) or sunny-side-up eggs (see page 53).

WATERCRESS SAUCE

3 handfuls (about 3 ounces/85 g) of watercress (tender stems are okay to include, but no roots!)

½ small shallot, coarsely chopped

2 tablespoons fresh lemon juice

1 tablespoon red wine vinegar

6 tablespoons (90 ml) extra-virgin olive oil

¼ teaspoon fine sea salt

Freshly ground black pepper

BASE

1 cup (200 g) French green lentils

1 yellow onion, cut in half and peeled

Fine sea salt

TOPPINGS

CRISPY MUSTARD CHICKEN

2 small boneless, skinless chicken breasts

(ingredients continue on next page)

⅓ cup (40 g) all-purpose flour

½ teaspoon fine sea salt

Freshly ground black pepper

1 large egg

1 tablespoon Dijon mustard

½ cup (55 g) plain dry breadcrumbs

¼ cup (25 g) finely grated Parmigiano-Reggiano cheese

1 tablespoon unsalted butter

1 tablespoon extra-virgin olive oil

1 handful (about 1 ounce/30 g) of baby spinach leaves

First, make the watercress sauce: In a blender, combine the watercress, shallot, lemon juice, vinegar, olive oil, salt, and several grinds of pepper. Blend until the watercress is finely chopped and the sauce is mostly smooth.

In a medium saucepan, place the lentils and onion and add about 1 quart (1 liter) of water and a few generous pinches of salt. Bring to a simmer and cook until the lentils are tender but still hold their shape, 20 to 25 minutes.

Meanwhile, put the chicken in a plastic bag or between 2 sheets of parchment paper and use a rolling pin or a meat tenderizer to pound the chicken to a little under ¼ inch (6 mm) thick. Don't be shy; this step requires a little muscle. In a shallow bowl, stir together the flour, salt, and several grinds of pepper. In another shallow bowl, beat the egg and mix in the mustard. In a third shallow bowl, stir together the breadcrumbs and Parmigiano. Coat each chicken breast with the flour mixture, then dunk it in the mustard-egg mixture, and then dredge it in the breadcrumb mixture, pressing to adhere the crumbs to all sides of the chicken.

Heat a large skillet over medium-high heat for 2 minutes. Add the butter and olive oil and swirl the skillet to evenly coat the surface. Add one chicken breast to the skillet and cook until browned on the first side, 2 to 4 minutes. Flip and cook on the second side until cooked through, another 2 to 4 minutes. Transfer the crispy chicken to a cutting board. Repeat with the other breast. You may need to add a little more oil to the skillet between batches.

When the lentils are done cooking, drain them and discard the onion. Return the lentils to their pot and stir in about half of the watercress sauce, saving the rest to serve alongside the finished bowl. Add the spinach leaves, stirring them in, and allow the residual heat from the lentils to wilt the spinach a little. Or, if you prefer, divide the lentils between 2 bowls and tuck the spinach leaves in among the lentils. Slice the crispy chicken and arrange on top of the lentils and spinach. Spoon on the remaining sauce or serve it on the side.

quinoa with sheet-pan salmon, see page 74

quinoa with sheet-pan salmon

quinoa base + roasted salmon + caramelized fennel and lemon wheels + lemon-shallot dressing

Serves 2 • This grain bowl works well on a busy weeknight because the salmon and fennel roast on the same sheet pan, making cleanup a breeze. In addition, if you cut a whole lemon and add it to the pan, the slices caramelize nicely in the hot oven. They look beautiful, and their sweet juice is delicious squeezed over the fish.

BASE

1½ cups (260 g) quinoa (any color), rinsed well

3 cups (720 ml) water

½ teaspoon fine sea salt

TOPPINGS

1 fennel bulb, cut into ½-inch (1 cm) slices, fronds reserved for garnish

1 whole lemon, cut into ½-inch (1 cm) slices, seeds discarded

2 tablespoons plus 2 teaspoons extra-virgin olive oil

Fine sea salt

Freshly ground black pepper

2 (6-ounce/170 g) salmon fillets

LEMON-SHALLOT DRESSING

2 tablespoons fresh lemon juice

½ small shallot, finely chopped

2 tablespoons extra-virgin olive oil

Fine sea salt

Heat the oven to 450°F (230°C).

In a small saucepan with a lid, combine the rinsed quinoa, water, and salt. Bring to a boil, then adjust the heat so that the water simmers gently. Cook, uncovered, until the quinoa has absorbed all of the water, 12 to 15 minutes. Remove the pan from the heat, cover with the lid, and let steam for 5 minutes. Fluff the quinoa with a fork before serving. Quinoa can be cooked ahead and stored, covered, in the fridge for up to 3 days.

While the quinoa is cooking, make the toppings: On a rimmed baking sheet, spread out the fennel and lemon slices. Drizzle with 2 tablespoons of the olive oil and season with ¼ teaspoon of salt and a few grinds of pepper. Roast until caramelized, 12 to 15 minutes.

Remove the baking sheet from the oven and decrease the oven temperature to 250°F (120°C).

Rub the salmon with the remaining 2 teaspoons oil and season with ¼ teaspoon of salt and several grinds of pepper. Flip the fennel and lemon on the sheet pan, make some room, and add the salmon. Roast until the fish is just barely cooked in the center and turns an opaque pink color, 6 to 12 minutes, depending on thickness.

While the salmon cooks, make the dressing: In a small bowl, whisk together the lemon juice, shallot, olive oil, and a big pinch of salt.

Divide the quinoa between 2 bowls and top with the salmon and fennel. Squeeze the juice from the lemon wheels over the fish. Garnish with the fennel fronds and drizzle the dressing over everything.

(g)rainbow

barley base + baby spinach + roasted rainbow vegetables + creamy tahini sauce + seven-minute eggs

Serves 2 ▪ Barley has a nutty flavor and a pleasant chewy texture. You'll find two types of barley at the grocery store: hulled and pearl. Pearl barley has been polished to remove the outer bran layer, so it's less nutritious than hulled barley, but it also cooks much faster. Use either kind in this recipe. The rainbow of vegetables in the ingredients list is just a suggestion. Feel free to substitute your favorites, keeping the total amount about the same and roasting just until tender.

BASE

Fine sea salt

1½ cups (300 g) barley (hulled or pearl)

TOPPINGS

10 to 12 small Brussels sprouts, cut in half

6 very small purple potatoes, cut in half

4 young carrots (each about 5 inches/13 cm long), chopped into bite-size pieces

1 shallot, peeled and cut in half lengthwise

2 tablespoons extra-virgin olive oil

½ teaspoon fine sea salt

¼ teaspoon freshly ground black pepper

2 handfuls (about 2 ounces/55 g) of baby spinach leaves

2 Seven-Minute Eggs (page 14)

Chopped flat-leaf parsley, for garnish

(ingredients continue on next page)

1 small garlic clove

Fine sea salt

¼ cup (70 g) tahini

1½ tablespoons fresh lemon juice

2 teaspoons honey

Freshly ground black pepper

2 tablespoons water

Heat the oven to 425°F (220°C).

Bring a large pot of generously salted water to a boil. Add the barley and decrease the heat to a gentle simmer. Cook, stirring occasionally, until the barley is chewy and tender, about 20 minutes for pearl barley and 40 minutes to 1 hour for hulled barley. Barley can be cooked ahead and stored covered in the fridge for 3 days.

Meanwhile, on a rimmed baking sheet, combine the Brussels sprouts, potatoes, carrots, and shallot. Drizzle with the olive oil and season with the salt and pepper. Mix well. Roast the vegetables, turning once or twice, until tender and dark brown in a few places, 30 to 40 minutes.

Use a mortar and pestle or the side of a large knife to crush the garlic and a pinch of salt into a paste. Transfer the garlic paste to a small bowl and whisk in the tahini, lemon juice, honey, and several grinds of pepper. While stirring continuously, gradually pour in the water. The mixture may seize at first, but continue whisking until the dressing is creamy and pourable. Taste and adjust the seasoning as needed.

When the barley is done cooking, drain it and divide it between 2 bowls. Arrange the roasted vegetables on top and scatter the baby spinach. Cut the eggs in half, season them with salt and pepper, and nestle two halves into each bowl. Drizzle the creamy tahini sauce over everything and garnish with the chopped parsley.

coconut farro with spicy sole

farro cooked in coconut milk base + spicy sole + chile crisp + cilantro + green onion

Serves 2 • Farro and other whole grains are easily cooked in plenty of salted water (as if you were boiling dried pasta), but they can also be cooked in more flavorful liquids like coconut milk. In this recipe, the coconut milk makes the farro base creamy and cooling, which is ideal because it's topped with spicy sole and the hot, crunchy condiment called chile crisp.

BASE

1 (13.5-ounce/400 ml) can of coconut milk

1½ cups (360 ml) water

1½ cups (200 g) farro, rinsed

1 teaspoon fine sea salt

TOPPINGS

2 (6-ounce/170 g) sole fillets

1 garlic clove, pounded into a paste

2 teaspoons chile crisp or chile oil with chile flakes in it, plus more for serving

3 tablespoons extra-virgin olive oil

¼ teaspoon fine sea salt

1 lime

½ cup (10 g) fresh cilantro leaves

1 green onion, white and green parts, thinly sliced

Make the base: In a medium saucepan, combine the coconut milk, water, farro, and salt. Bring to a gentle simmer and cook, stirring occasionally, until the farro is tender and has absorbed almost all of the liquid and has a creamy texture similar to risotto or rice pudding, 15 to 30 minutes, depending on the type of farro. If the farro is still crunchy and needs to cook longer but has already absorbed all of the liquid, pour in a little more water as needed and continue cooking until tender. Taste and season with a little more salt if needed.

Heat the oven to 425°F (220°C). Line a baking sheet with foil.

Place the sole fillets on the prepared baking sheet, skin-side up if the fish has skin. In a small bowl, stir together the garlic, chile crisp, and oil. Rub the spicy mixture all over the fish. Season the fillets evenly with the salt. Roast until the fish is just barely cooked in the center and turns an opaque white color, 8 to 10 minutes. As soon as you pull the fish out of the oven, finely grate some lime zest over it and reserve the zested lime for serving alongside the fish.

Divide the farro between 2 bowls. Place the roasted sole on top, then garnish with the cilantro and green onion. Squeeze the lime and spoon a little of the pan juices over the greens, and serve with extra chile crisp, if you like.

tabbouleh, hold the greens

bulgur and crispy chickpea base + pomegranate seeds + radish + feta +

mint + pomegranate molasses vinaigrette

Serves 2 · Tabbouleh is a Levantine grain salad traditionally made with bulgur and lots of finely chopped parsley. In this not-at-all-authentic variation, there's no parsley, but there are crispy roasted chickpeas, thinly sliced radishes, pomegranate seeds, and feta crumbles, plus a sweet-tart pomegranate molasses vinaigrette that ties everything together.

BASE

1 (15-ounce/425 g) can of chickpeas, drained and rinsed

4 tablespoons (60 ml) extra-virgin olive oil

Fine sea salt

Freshly ground black pepper

1½ cups (285 g) fine or coarse bulgur

1 cup (240 ml) boiling water

POMEGRANATE MOLASSES VINAIGRETTE

1 tablespoon pomegranate molasses

2 teaspoons red wine vinegar

1 teaspoon honey

Fine sea salt

Freshly ground black pepper

3 tablespoons extra-virgin olive oil

(ingredients continue on next page)

other grains and legumes   83

½ cup (90 g) pomegranate seeds

4 radishes, very thinly sliced

3 mint sprigs, leaves very thinly sliced

2 ounces (55 g) feta, crumbled

Heat the oven to 400°F (200°C).

On a rimmed baking sheet, spread out the chickpeas, drizzle with 2 tablespoons of the olive oil, and season with ¼ teaspoon of salt and several grinds of pepper. Mix well. Roast, stirring once or twice, until the chickpeas are dark golden brown and crisp, about 20 minutes.

Meanwhile, in a small bowl, mix together the bulgur, the remaining 2 tablespoons oil, and a big pinch of salt, stirring until the grains are coated with the oil. Pour the boiling water over the bulgur and immediately cover the bowl tightly with plastic wrap. Let rest for at least 15 minutes while you make the pomegranate molasses vinaigrette and prepare the toppings.

For the vinaigrette, in a small bowl, whisk together the pomegranate molasses, vinegar, honey, a pinch of salt, and several grinds of pepper. Gradually pour in the oil and stir until emulsified.

Uncover the bulgur, fluff it with a fork, and divide between 2 bowls. Divide the roasted chickpeas between the bowls as well. Top with the pomegranate seeds, radish slices, mint, and feta. Drizzle the pomegranate molasses vinaigrette over everything.

smoked salmon on rye

rye berries base + smoked salmon + creamy dill-juniper sauce

Serves 2 ▪ Rye berries have a subtly sweet malt flavor (just like rye bread) that goes perfectly with smoked salmon. Look for them in the bulk bins at natural foods stores. If you happen to have any Pickled Pink Onions (page 117) on hand, scatter a few on top of this bowl for a tart crunch.

BASE

Fine sea salt

1½ cups (270 g) rye berries

2 tablespoons extra-virgin olive oil

CREAMY DILL-JUNIPER SAUCE

6 juniper berries

1 small garlic clove

¼ cup (60 g) crème fraîche

¼ cup (5 g) fresh dill, finely chopped, plus 6 small sprigs for garnish

2 tablespoons fresh lemon juice

Fine sea salt

Freshly ground black pepper

TOPPINGS

3 ounces (85 g) sliced smoked salmon

Freshly ground black pepper

For the base, bring a medium pot of salted water to a boil. Add the rye berries and simmer, uncovered, until chewy and tender, about 1 hour. Rye berries can be cooked ahead and stored, covered, in the fridge for up to 3 days. Reheat them before serving.

Meanwhile, make the sauce: Using a mortar and pestle or the side of a large knife, crush the juniper berries and garlic into a smooth paste. In a small bowl, whisk together the crème fraîche, dill, lemon juice, and the juniper-garlic paste. Whisk for at least 1 minute, until the mixture thickens (like softly whipped cream). Taste and season with salt and lots of pepper. Set aside in the fridge until needed.

When the rye berries are done cooking, drain them thoroughly and then return them to the pot and stir in the olive oil. Divide the rye berries between 2 bowls. Spoon in the dill-juniper sauce and arrange the smoked salmon on top, fanning out the slices. Garnish each bowl with a few fresh dill sprigs and some freshly ground pepper.

noodles

sesame soba

soba noodle base	+	crispy salt-and-pepper tofu	+	broccolini	+	black sesame seeds	+	sesame seed sauce

Serves 2 • Tossing just-boiled soba noodles with a small amount of sesame oil helps prevent them from sticking together and adds a boost of sesame flavor, too. If you can't find Broccolini at the market, use the same amount of regular broccoli instead and cut it into 1-inch (2.5 cm) florets, slicing in half lengthwise if the stems are thicker than your thumb.

TOPPINGS

BROCCOLINI

Fine sea salt

1 bunch (6 ounces/170 g) of Broccolini, lower stems trimmed, cut into 3-inch (7.5 cm) pieces

CRISPY SALT-AND-PEPPER TOFU

3 tablespoons vegetable oil

10 ounces (285 g) firm tofu, patted dry and cut into 1-inch (2.5 cm) cubes

¼ teaspoon fine sea salt

¼ teaspoon freshly ground black pepper

1 green onion, white and green parts, thinly sliced for garnish

Black or white sesame seeds

BASE

6 ounces (170 g) soba noodles

1½ teaspoons sesame oil

SESAME SEED SAUCE

1 large garlic clove, finely grated or crushed into a paste

1-inch (2.5 cm) piece of ginger, peeled and finely grated

(ingredients continue on next page)

1 teaspoon light or dark brown sugar

2 tablespoons tahini or Chinese sesame paste

1 tablespoon soy sauce or tamari

1 tablespoon rice vinegar

Bring a large pot of generously salted water to a boil. Add the Broccolini to the boiling water and cook until bright green and tender but still crunchy, 1 to 2 minutes. Use tongs to transfer the Broccolini to a colander and let it drain.

In the same pot of boiling water, cook the soba noodles until al dente, following the instructions on the package. Scoop up about ½ cup (120 ml) of cooking water and set aside. Drain the soba noodles, then, in a large bowl, toss them with the sesame oil.

For the crispy tofu, heat a large skillet over medium-high heat for 1 minute. Pour in the vegetable oil, swirling to coat the entire skillet. Carefully add the tofu cubes in a single layer. Sprinkle with the salt and pepper and cook, without moving the tofu, until the undersides are golden brown and crisp, 4 to 5 minutes. Flip and cook on the opposite side for 2 to 3 minutes. (If the tofu cubes stick to the skillet when you try to flip them, give them another minute and try again.) Transfer the tofu to a plate and let cool while you make the sauce.

To the bowl of soba noodles, add the garlic, ginger, brown sugar, tahini, soy sauce, vinegar, and 6 tablespoons (90 ml) of the reserved cooking water. Mix until the noodles are evenly coated. Add a little more of the reserved water, 1 tablespoon at a time, until the sauce coats the noodles generously and even pools a tiny bit in the bottom of the bowl.

Divide the soba noodles between 2 bowls, top with the Broccolini and crispy tofu, and scatter the green onion and sesame seeds over everything.

chicken paprikash

buttered egg noodle base	+	saucy chicken	+	sour cream	+	parsley

Serves 2 • This bowl is pure comfort on a chilly day. It's all about soft textures: buttered egg noodles, succulent braised chicken in tomato sauce, and a big dollop of sour cream. You can make the saucy chicken ahead of time and reheat it before serving for an easy lunch or dinner.

TOPPINGS

SAUCY CHICKEN

2 or 3 large bone-in, skin-on chicken thighs

Fine sea salt

Freshly ground black pepper

1 tablespoon unsalted butter

½ small yellow onion, finely chopped

3 garlic cloves, sliced

1 tablespoon all-purpose flour

3 tablespoons smoked sweet paprika

1 (15-ounce/425 g) can of diced tomatoes

1 cup (240 ml) water

¼ cup (60 g) sour cream or crème fraîche

¼ cup (5 g) fresh flat-leaf parsley, chopped

BASE

Fine sea salt

8 ounces (225 g) egg noodles

1 tablespoon unsalted butter

Freshly ground black pepper

Heat the oven to 350°F (180°C).

Make the saucy chicken: Pat the chicken dry with paper towels. Season with ¼ teaspoon of salt and several grinds of pepper. In a medium or large oven-safe skillet, melt the butter over medium-high heat. Place the chicken skin-side down in the skillet and cook until the skin is dark golden brown, 6 to 8 minutes. Use tongs to transfer the chicken to a plate, skin-side up. (It won't be fully cooked yet because it's going to cook further in the tomato sauce.)

Pour off all but about 2 tablespoons of fat into a small bowl and set aside. Return the pan with the remaining fat to medium heat. Add the onion, garlic, and ¼ teaspoon of salt and cook, stirring occasionally with a wooden spoon, until the vegetables are softened and starting to brown, 4 to 6 minutes. Use the spoon to push the onion and garlic to the side of the pan and create a little empty space in the middle. Pour 1 tablespoon of the reserved fat into the empty space and add the flour and paprika. Immediately stir to mix everything together in the pan, being careful to not burn the paprika. Stir in the tomatoes, water, and ¾ teaspoon of salt. Nestle the browned chicken in the pan, skin-side up, and pour in any juices that have settled on the plate. Transfer the skillet to the oven and cook until the sauce thickens and the chicken is cooked through, 25 to 35 minutes.

While the chicken is cooking, bring a medium pot of generously salted water to a boil. Add the egg noodles and cook until al dente, about 7 minutes. Drain the noodles, return them to the pot, and stir in the butter. Taste and season lightly with salt and pepper.

Divide the buttered noodles between 2 bowls. Top each bowl with a chicken thigh and plenty of the tomato sauce. Dollop the sour cream alongside the chicken and sprinkle the chopped parsley over everything.

pad thai

rice noodle base + shrimp + egg + bean sprouts + toasted peanuts +

lime + tamarind sauce

Serves 2 • Proper pad Thai should have tang from tamarind and lime juice, plus saltiness and funkiness from fish sauce, and just a hint of sweetness from sugar. You can make it spicy by topping it with as much ground chile powder as you like. For vegetarian pad Thai, omit the shrimp and fish sauce (and add some salt or soy sauce in its place).

BASE

7 ounces (200 g) dried rice noodles

2 large eggs

6 medium or large raw shrimp (about 8 ounces/225 g), peeled and deveined, tails left on, patted dry

1 cup (100 g) bean sprouts

¼ cup (35 g) salted toasted peanuts (see page 15), coarsely chopped, plus more for garnish

3 tablespoons chopped garlic chives (optional)

3 tablespoons vegetable oil

TOPPINGS

Ground chile powder

Lime wedges

TAMARIND SAUCE

2 tablespoons water

1 tablespoon tamarind paste

1 tablespoon light or dark brown sugar

1 tablespoon fresh lime juice

1 tablespoon fish sauce

Set a kettle or small saucepan filled with water on the stove and bring to a boil. Place the rice noodles in a large bowl. Pour in enough boiling water to cover and let soak until the noodles are tender but not mushy, about 15 minutes, stirring once or twice to prevent the noodles from sticking to each other.

While the rice noodles are soaking, prep your other ingredients and make the sauce. In a small bowl, beat the 2 eggs together, and make sure the shrimp, bean sprouts, peanuts, and garlic chives, if using, are prepared. Keep all these ingredients next to the stove, ready to go.

To make the sauce, stir together the water, tamarind paste, brown sugar, lime juice, and fish sauce.

Drain the noodles.

Heat a large skillet over high heat for 3 minutes. Swirl in the vegetable oil. Add the shrimp and cook on the first side for 30 seconds, then flip and cook on the second side for 30 seconds. Stir in the noodles, coating them in the oil, then pour in the sauce. Cook, stirring constantly, for 1 minute. Push the noodles to one side of the skillet and add the eggs to the other side. Cook the eggs, stirring, until they scramble, about 30 seconds. Add the bean sprouts, peanuts, and garlic chives, if using, and mix everything together in the pan. Cook and stir for 1 minute more, then divide the pad Thai between 2 bowls. Garnish with additional peanuts, a big pinch or two of ground chile, and lime wedges.

sicilian favorites

ziti pasta base + caponata-style tomato sauce + ricotta salata + toasted pine nuts + parsley

Serves 2 • Caponata is a Sicilian dish made from fried eggplant cubes, chopped tomatoes and celery, and sweetened vinegar. Traditionally, caponata is served on its own, but here it serves as a full-flavored sauce for a noodle bowl that's topped with a few other Sicilian ingredients. This recipe makes a little more caponata than you'll need; leftovers are delicious spooned on toast with a drizzle of olive oil.

CAPONATA-STYLE TOMATO SAUCE

1 eggplant (about 1 pound/455 g), cut into 1-inch (2.5 cm) cubes

5 tablespoons (75 ml) extra-virgin olive oil

Fine sea salt

Freshly ground black pepper

½ yellow onion, chopped

1 celery stalk, chopped

2 garlic cloves, sliced

1 tablespoon capers, rinsed

1 tablespoon red wine vinegar

2 teaspoons sugar

1 (15-ounce/425 g) can of diced tomatoes

BASE

Fine sea salt

8 ounces (225 g) dried ziti or rigatoni pasta

1 tablespoon extra-virgin olive oil

TOPPINGS

Ricotta salata cheese, freshly shaved with a vegetable peeler

2 tablespoons toasted pine nuts (see page 15)

¼ cup (5 g) fresh flat-leaf parsley, chopped

Chile flakes, for garnish (optional)

Heat the oven to 400°F (200°C).

Make the sauce: Place the eggplant cubes on a rimmed baking sheet, toss with 3 tablespoons of the olive oil, and season with ¼ teaspoon of salt and several grinds of pepper. Roast the eggplant, turning once or twice, until golden brown and tender, about 25 minutes. When finished cooking, remove the eggplant from the oven and set aside.

While the eggplant roasts, heat the remaining 2 tablespoons oil in a large nonreactive pan (i.e. *not* aluminum, cast iron, or unlined copper) over medium heat. Add the onion, celery, garlic, and capers. Cook, stirring occasionally, until the vegetables are softened, about 5 minutes. Stir in the vinegar, sugar, tomatoes, and ¼ teaspoon of salt. Simmer gently until the sauce thickens and the flavors come together, about 8 minutes. Taste and season with a little more salt and pepper. Stir the roasted eggplant cubes into the sauce.

Bring a medium pot of generously salted water to a boil. Add the pasta and cook until al dente, about 7 minutes. Reserve 1 cup (240 ml) of the pasta cooking water, then drain the pasta and return it directly to the pot. Add the olive oil and a splash of the reserved cooking water and stir to coat the noodles. You can use a splash of the remaining cooking water to thin the sauce, if you like.

Divide the pasta between 2 bowls. Top with some caponata-style sauce. (Alternatively, add the cooked noodles directly to the pan of sauce and toss together over medium heat for a few minutes, until the sauce cloaks the pasta.) Scatter the ricotta salata, toasted pine nuts, and parsley over the pasta and garnish with a pinch or two of chile flakes, if you like.

vegan ramen

ramen noodle base + miso–shiitake mushroom broth + enoki mushrooms + pea shoots

+ watermelon radish + shichimi togarashi + nori

Serves 2 • You won't miss the porkiness of regular ramen broth here because the miso–shiitake mushroom broth is just as flavorful. If you'd like to add protein, cubes of tofu would be fantastic swimming in the broth. Or, for a vegetarian version, should you be so inclined, you could add a very nonvegan Seven-Minute Egg (page 14) to each serving. All the toppings are flexible—feel free to use your favorites.

MISO–SHIITAKE MUSHROOM BROTH

½ yellow onion, chopped

1 tablespoon vegetable oil

2 garlic cloves, sliced

1-inch (2.5 cm) piece of ginger, peeled and finely grated

1 tablespoon white miso paste

2 cups (480 ml) mushroom stock or vegetable stock

2 cups (480 ml) water

1 ounce (30 g) dried shiitake mushrooms, broken into small pieces

1 piece of kombu seaweed

1 tablespoon mirin or rice vinegar

Soy sauce or tamari, as needed

BASE

Fine sea salt

2 (3-ounce/85 g or 4-ounce/ 115 g) packages of dried ramen noodles (vegan or made with egg)

TOPPINGS

1 handful (about 3 ounces/85 g) of enoki mushrooms

(ingredients continue on next page)

2 teaspoons sesame oil

2 handfuls (about 2 ounces/55 g) of pea shoots or sunflower shoots

1 watermelon radish, thinly sliced

1 green onion, white and green parts, thinly sliced

1 sheet of nori, torn into 4 strips

Toasted sesame seeds

Shichimi togarashi

Chile oil or chile crisp

Make the broth: In a medium pot, cook the onion in the vegetable oil over medium-high heat, stirring often, until dark golden brown in some places, about 7 minutes. Add the garlic, ginger, and miso. Cook, stirring, for 1 minute, lowering the heat if needed to prevent the garlic from burning. Pour in the stock and water. Add the shiitake mushrooms, kombu, and mirin. Once the mixture comes to a boil, adjust the heat to a very gentle simmer and cook for 30 minutes. Use tongs to remove and discard the kombu. Taste the broth and add a splash of soy sauce if you'd like the broth to be saltier. You can strain the broth, if you want, or you can leave as is. Keep the broth warm on the stove until you're ready to serve.

Bring a medium pot of salted water to a boil. Cook the ramen noodles according to the instructions on the package. Drain the noodles and transfer to 2 bowls. Cook the enoki mushrooms in the sesame oil in a skillet over medium-high heat until the mushrooms soften a little and turn very light golden brown, about 3 minutes. Divide them between the bowls.

Top with the pea shoots, sliced radish, and green onion. Tuck a couple of nori strips on the side of each bowl. Ladle in the miso–shiitake broth. Garnish with a sprinkle of sesame seeds and shichimi togarashi and a tiny drizzle of chile oil.

pasta e piselli

pappardelle pasta and green peas base	+	pea shoot salad	+	crispy pancetta crumbs	+	Parmigiano

Serves 2 · Everything in this bowl happens to begin with the letter *P*: pappardelle, peas, pea shoots, pancetta, and Parmigiano. It was not intentional, but now the rule is if you're going to add any other toppings, they need to be *P* foods. Just kidding!

BASE

Fine sea salt

8 ounces (225 g) dried pappardelle pasta (or any shape)

2 garlic cloves, sliced

1½ cups (225 g) shelled fresh or frozen peas

2 tablespoons unsalted butter

TOPPINGS

PANCETTA CRUMBS

4 ounces (115 g) meaty pancetta, finely chopped

PEA SHOOT SALAD

2 handfuls (about 2 ounces/55 g) of pea shoots or other fresh tender greens such as arugula, watercress, or baby spinach leaves

½ lemon

Flaky sea salt

Freshly ground black pepper

Extra-virgin olive oil

Parmigiano-Reggiano cheese, freshly shaved with a vegetable peeler, for garnish

Make the pasta base: Bring a large pot of generously salted water to a boil. When the water is boiling, add the pasta and cook until al dente, about 7 minutes.

While waiting for the water to come to a boil, line a plate with paper towels or a clean brown paper bag and set aside. In a large skillet, cook the pancetta over medium heat, stirring occasionally, until crisp and browned, 7 to 10 minutes. Use tongs or a wooden spoon to transfer the pancetta to the prepared plate to drain, reserving the fat in the skillet.

Return the skillet to medium heat. Add the garlic and cook, stirring constantly, until light golden brown, about 1 minute. Remove the skillet from the heat.

When the pasta is done, reserve 1 cup (240 ml) of the pasta cooking water, then drain the pasta and transfer it directly to the skillet. Set the skillet over medium-high heat, add the peas, butter, and half of the reserved pasta water, and cook, stirring vigorously, until the sauce emulsifies and coats the noodles, 1 to 2 minutes. (There should be a little liquid pooling in the skillet. If not, add more pasta water until you've got a light sauce.)

For the pea shoot topping, in a medium bowl, toss the pea shoots with a generous squeeze of lemon juice, a pinch of flaky salt, and several grinds of pepper.

Divide the pasta between 2 serving bowls. Pile the pea shoot salad on top of the pasta, drizzle lightly with olive oil, and scatter the crispy pancetta crumbs over everything. Garnish with lots of Parmigiano.

greens

not-leafy caesar

thinly sliced fennel base + anchovy croutons + seven-minute eggs + garlicky dressing

Serves 2 • Classic Caesar salad is turned on its head in this not-leafy version with anchovy croutons and soft-boiled eggs. In place of fennel, you could try thinly sliced radishes or a combination of the two. You'll have some extra aioli from the dressing, but that's a very good problem to have; use it on a sandwich or as a dip for oven fries.

BASE

2 medium fennel bulbs, sliced as thinly as possible, plus chopped fronds for garnish

TOPPINGS

ANCHOVY CROUTONS

2 thick slices of country-style bread (like rustic sourdough)

3 tablespoons extra-virgin olive oil

2 anchovy fillets, rinsed, patted dry, and very finely chopped

2 Seven-Minute Eggs (page 14)

Flaky sea salt

Freshly ground black pepper

Parmigiano-Reggiano cheese, freshly shaved with a vegetable peeler, for garnish

GARLICKY DRESSING

2 or 3 small garlic cloves

Fine sea salt

1 egg yolk

¾ cup (180 ml) extra-virgin olive oil

½ lemon

1 anchovy fillet, rinsed and patted dry

Freshly ground black pepper

Place the thinly sliced fennel in a large bowl and set aside.

Make the anchovy croutons: Tear the bread into irregularly shaped 1½-inch (4 cm) pieces. Heat a large pan over medium-high heat. Add 2 tablespoons of the olive oil and the bread pieces. Cook, stirring often, until the bread is golden brown in a few places, about 3 minutes. Add the chopped anchovies and the remaining 1 tablespoon oil and continue cooking till the croutons are crisp on the outside, 2 to 3 minutes more. Transfer the anchovy croutons to the bowl of fennel.

For the dressing, start by making aioli: Using a mortar and pestle or the side of a large knife, crush the garlic and 2 or 3 pinches of salt into a smooth paste. In a medium bowl, whisk the egg yolk to break it up. While whisking continuously, add a few drops of the olive oil. Whisk until fully incorporated, then add a few more drops of oil. Continue whisking and adding the oil by the drop until the mixture thickens, looks sticky, and pulls away from the sides of the bowl. While whisking continuously, add a little more oil, this time in a very thin and slow stream. Once you've added somewhere between one-third and one-half the total oil, squeeze in a little lemon juice to thin the aioli. Add the remaining oil, still in a very thin and slow stream while whisking continuously. The aioli should be as thick as mayonnaise. If it's thin and watery, it broke—whoops! Don't worry, this happens to the best of us, and you can easily fix broken aioli. Start with a fresh egg yolk in a clean bowl. Follow the recipe as outlined above, but instead of adding oil to the egg yolk, add the broken aioli mixture (first drop by drop and then in a very thin and slow stream) while whisking continuously. I find it most helpful to transfer the broken aioli mixture to a liquid measuring cup or something with a pour spout.

Stir the garlic paste into the aioli. Taste and adjust the seasoning, adding more salt and lemon juice if needed. Transfer about ⅓ cup (80 ml) of the aioli to a small bowl and store the remaining aioli in an airtight container in the refrigerator for up to 2 days. Use the mortar and pestle again (no need to clean it out after crushing the garlic) or the side of a large knife to pound the anchovy into a smooth paste. Stir the anchovy paste into the aioli along with a big squeeze of lemon juice and lots of pepper. Drizzle the dressing over the fennel and anchovy croutons and use your hands to toss gently.

Cut the eggs in half and season them with flaky salt and pepper. Divide the dressed salad and the eggs between 2 bowls. Top with the Parmigiano and fennel fronds.

scandinavian salad

arugula base	+	tarragon cream sauce	+	smoked trout	+	pickled pink onions

Serves 2 • Smoked trout is underrated. Salmon gets all the love, but trout has fantastic flavor and comes in a variety of colors. Brook trout and steelhead are vivid orange, while rainbow trout is more of a pearly pink color, despite its name. Use any smoked trout for this Scandinavian-inspired bowl, and consider making a double batch of the pickled pink onions. They're good on pretty much everything!

TOPPINGS

PICKLED PINK ONIONS

¾ cup (180 ml) rice vinegar, apple cider vinegar, or white wine vinegar

¾ cup (180 ml) water

1 tablespoon sugar

1½ teaspoons fine sea salt

4 black peppercorns

1 small or medium red onion, thinly sliced crosswise into rings

3 ounces (85 g) smoked trout, flaked

TARRAGON CREAM SAUCE

1 small garlic clove

Fine sea salt

1 teaspoon fresh tarragon leaves

5 tablespoons (75 g) crème fraîche

1 teaspoon fresh lemon juice

Freshly ground black pepper

BASE

3 handfuls (about 3 ounces/85 g) of arugula

½ lemon

Extra-virgin olive oil

Flaky sea salt

Freshly ground black pepper

First, make the pickled pink onions: In a small nonreactive pot (i.e. *not* aluminum, cast iron, or unlined copper), combine the vinegar, water, sugar, salt, and peppercorns. Bring to a boil. Add the onion slices, remove the pot from the heat, and let the onions pickle in the pot until cool, about 1 hour. Pickled pink onions can be enjoyed immediately or transferred with some of their brine to a 1-pint (480 ml) jar, covered with a lid, and stored in the fridge for up to 3 weeks.

For the tarragon cream sauce, use a mortar and pestle or the side of a large knife to crush the garlic and a big pinch of fine salt into a smooth paste. Crush or finely chop the tarragon leaves as well to muddle them. Transfer the garlic paste and crushed tarragon to a small bowl and stir in the crème fraîche and lemon juice. Taste and season with more fine salt and lots of pepper.

In a large bowl, toss the arugula with a squeeze of lemon juice, a drizzle of oil (enough to lightly coat but not weigh down the leaves), and a pinch each of flaky salt and pepper.

Divide the dressed arugula between 2 bowls. Top with the smoked trout and a few pickled pink onions. Spoon a dollop of tarragon cream sauce into each bowl.

salade niçoise

chicories base + haricots verts + tuna + Niçoise olives + new potatoes + Dijon vinaigrette

Serves 2 • This colorful bowl tastes best when you use ripe produce at the peak of its season. Look for the slender French green beans called haricots verts, but if you can't find them, substitute a sliced heirloom tomato, use a few extra potatoes, or just leave them out entirely.

BASE

½ small head of radicchio, torn into bite-size leaves

2 Belgian endives, separated into individual leaves

TOPPINGS

Fine sea salt

4 small (about 7 ounces/200 g) red or yellow potatoes, halved

4 ounces (115 g) haricots verts, stem ends trimmed (you can leave their little tails)

2 Seven-Minute Eggs (page 14)

Flaky sea salt

Freshly ground black pepper

¼ cup (1 ounce/30 g) pitted Niçoise olives

1 (5-ounce/140 g) can of olive oil–packed tuna, drained and flaked

DIJON VINAIGRETTE

1 small garlic clove

Fine sea salt

2 tablespoons fresh lemon juice

1 teaspoon red wine vinegar

Freshly ground black pepper

Dijon mustard

3 tablespoons extra-virgin olive oil

Place the radicchio and endive leaves in a large bowl and set aside.

Bring a small pot of generously salted water to a boil. Add the potatoes and cook until they are tender when poked with a fork, about 15 minutes. Use a slotted spoon to transfer the boiled potatoes to a plate.

Add the haricots verts to the same pot of boiling water. Cook the beans until bright green and tender but still a little crunchy, 1½ minutes. Drain and transfer the beans to the plate with the potatoes.

Make the Dijon vinaigrette: Using a mortar and pestle or the side of a large knife, crush the garlic and a pinch of salt into a smooth paste. Transfer to a small bowl and stir in the lemon juice, vinegar, another ¼ teaspoon of salt, and several grinds of pepper. Dip the tines of a clean fork into the mustard jar. When you lift the fork, a small amount of mustard should cling to the tines. Dunk the fork into the lemon juice mixture and stir to incorporate. Pour in the olive oil and stir until emulsified.

Pour half of the dressing over the radicchio and endive and toss gently with your hands until the leaves are evenly coated. Cut the eggs in half and season them with flaky salt and pepper.

Divide the dressed chicory leaves between 2 serving bowls. Arrange the boiled potatoes and haricots verts on one side of the bowl and the olives and tuna on the other side. Nestle the egg halves in the bowls. Drizzle the remaining dressing over the potatoes and haricots verts.

antipasto, see page 124

antipasto

romaine
lettuce base
+
cured
meats
+
cheese
+
pickled
vegetables
+
Italian-style
dressing

Serves 2 · You can customize this chopped Italian salad to include all your favorite ingredients. For instance, choose a mix of cured meats instead of the spicy soppressata and mortadella—just make sure to keep the total amount about the same. Olives of any kind could also stand in for the pickled peppers.

BASE

1 small head (12 ounces/340 g) of romaine lettuce, any bruised outer leaves discarded, chopped

¼ small head of radicchio, very thinly sliced (optional)

ITALIAN-STYLE DRESSING

1 small garlic clove

¼ teaspoon fine sea salt

1 tablespoon red wine vinegar

1 tablespoon fresh lemon juice

½ teaspoon dried oregano

3 tablespoons extra-virgin olive oil

Freshly ground black pepper

TOPPINGS

2½ ounces (70 g) mozzarella cheese, cut into ½-inch (1 cm) cubes

1 ounce (30 g) sliced soppressata, cut into ribbons ¼ inch (6 mm) wide

2 ounces (55 g) sliced mortadella, cut into ribbons ½ inch (1 cm) wide

⅓ cup (85 g) marinated artichoke hearts

¼ cup (45 g) pickled mild peppers

¼ cup (60 g) fresh ricotta cheese

Place the chopped romaine and radicchio in a large bowl and set aside.

To make the dressing, use a mortar and pestle or the side of a large knife to crush the garlic and salt into a paste. Transfer the garlic paste to a medium bowl and whisk in the vinegar, lemon juice, and oregano. While whisking continuously, slowly pour in the olive oil. Season with lots of pepper.

Add the dressing to the lettuces and toss until the leaves are evenly coated. Divide the salad between 2 bowls. Top with the mozzarella, soppressata, mortadella, artichoke hearts, and pickled peppers. Nestle spoonfuls of the ricotta among the other toppings.

panzanella caprese

mixed baby greens base + tomatoes + torn croutons + mozzarella + basil

Serves 2 • If you like caprese (mozzarella, tomatoes, and basil), then you'll love this mash-up of caprese and another classic Italian dish. Panzanella is bread salad, which sounds like an oxymoron but is, in fact, a brilliant way to use up day-old bread or croutons. By mixing juicy ripe tomatoes with bread, you revive the bread and imbue it with extra flavor at the same time.

BASE

4 handfuls (about 4 ounces/115 g) of mixed baby greens

Flaky sea salt

Freshly ground black pepper

TOPPINGS

TORN CROUTONS

2 thick slices of country-style bread (like rustic sourdough)

2 tablespoons extra-virgin olive oil

¼ teaspoon fine sea salt

12 ounces (340 g) ripe tomatoes (a mix of colors is nice!)

2 teaspoons red wine vinegar

½ teaspoon flaky sea salt

Freshly ground black pepper

4 ounces (115 g) fresh mozzarella or burrata cheese

8 large fresh basil leaves, thinly sliced into ribbons or torn into small pieces

Good-quality extra-virgin olive oil

Divide the mixed greens between 2 serving bowls and season them with a big pinch of flaky salt and several grinds of pepper.

For the croutons, tear the bread into irregularly shaped 1½-inch (4 cm) pieces. Heat a large pan over medium-high heat. Add the olive oil, bread pieces, and salt. Cook, stirring often, until the croutons are golden brown in a few places and crisp on the outside, 4 to 8 minutes.

Meanwhile, slice the tomatoes into bite-size wedges and place them in a large bowl along with the vinegar, flaky salt, and lots of pepper. Using a large spoon, gently crush the tomatoes to release some of their juices.

When the croutons are done cooking, transfer them to the bowl with the tomatoes. Mix well, then place the tomato-bread salad on top of each bowl of greens.

Slice or tear the mozzarella into bite-size pieces and add them to the bowls. Scatter the basil on top of everything. Drizzle generously with olive oil.

shrimp taco salad

green cabbage base + tomato rice + chipotle shrimp + tortilla chips +

crispy pepitas + avocado + lime

Serves 2 • Reimagining your favorite dish, such as shrimp tacos, as individual components is a winning strategy to crafting a delicious bowl. Green cabbage makes up the base of this bowl along with a scoop of tomato rice to fill you up. Smoky-spicy shrimp, avocado, crispy pepitas, and homemade tortilla chips are all toppings. You can definitely use store-bought tortilla chips if you don't want to make your own.

BASE

½ small head of green cabbage, cored, sliced as thinly as possible

2 limes, halved

2 tablespoons extra-virgin olive oil

¼ teaspoon fine sea salt

TOMATO RICE

2 tablespoons vegetable oil

½ cup (100 g) long-grain white rice

1 tablespoon tomato paste

½ small yellow onion, finely chopped

1 large tomato, finely chopped

1 large or 2 small garlic cloves, minced

¼ teaspoon cumin seeds

½ teaspoon fine sea salt

1 cup (240 ml) chicken broth or water

(ingredients continue on next page)

TOPPINGS

TORTILLA CHIPS

6 tablespoons (90 ml) vegetable oil

4 small corn tortillas, sliced into strips ½ inch (1 cm) wide

Flaky sea salt

CRISPY PEPITAS

¼ cup (30 g) hulled pumpkin seeds (aka pepitas)

CHIPOTLE SHRIMP

6 to 9 medium or large raw shrimp (8 to 12 ounces/225 to 340 g), peeled and deveined, tails left on

1 teaspoon cornstarch

¼ teaspoon chipotle chile powder or smoked paprika

¼ teaspoon fine sea salt

½ avocado, sliced

Fresh cilantro leaves, for garnish (optional)

In a large bowl, combine the sliced cabbage with the juice of both limes, the olive oil, and fine salt. Use your hands to toss well.

Make the tomato rice: Heat the vegetable oil in a medium saucepan with a lid over medium heat. Add the rice and cook, stirring, until toasted and golden, 3 to 5 minutes. Stir in the tomato paste, onion, and chopped tomato and cook until the onion softens and the tomato juices thicken a little, 2 to 3 minutes. Add the garlic, cumin, and fine salt. Cook, stirring constantly, until the garlic is fragrant but not at all browned, 30 seconds. Pour in the broth. Decrease the heat to medium-low, cover the pot, and cook for about 15 minutes, until all the liquid has been absorbed by the rice. Remove the lid and fluff the tomato rice with a fork.

While the tomato rice cooks, you can make the toppings. Line a plate with paper towels or a clean brown paper bag and set aside. In a heavy-bottomed skillet, heat the vegetable oil over medium-high heat for 2 minutes. Slide one tortilla strip into the hot oil to check if it's hot enough—if the tortilla immediately sputters and begins to fry, the oil is ready. Add half the tortilla strips to the skillet so as not to overcrowd the pan and cook, stirring to turn them and keep separated, until golden and crisp, 3 to 4 minutes. Use tongs to transfer the tortilla chips to the prepared plate to drain. Sprinkle them with flaky salt. Repeat to fry the other tortilla strips, decreasing the heat if the tortillas are browning too quickly.

Add the pepitas to the hot oil in the skillet and cook, stirring constantly, until crisp, about 1 minute. Use a slotted spoon to transfer the crispy pepitas to the plate with the tortilla chips. Remove the skillet from the heat and discard all but 2 tablespoons of the oil.

Place the shrimp in a large bowl and sprinkle with the cornstarch, chipotle chile powder, and fine salt. Mix well. Return the skillet with the oil to medium-high heat. Add the seasoned shrimp and cook, using tongs to flip the shrimp once, until just barely opaque, 2 to 3 minutes. (You can cut off their tails before adding them to the bowl, if you prefer, but I like to leave them on because they're beautiful. If you serve them tails on, consider setting each place with a knife, or you can always just use your hands to pick up the shrimp.)

Divide the dressed cabbage and tomato rice between 2 bowls and top with the chipotle shrimp, tortilla chips, crispy pepitas, avocado, and cilantro, if using.

shrimp taco salad, see page 129

SOURCES

There aren't any recipes in this book that require specific brands of ingredients. But if you're looking for a little direction in terms of finding store-bought ingredients, here are some favorite producers to keep your eye out for.

ANCHOVIES AND OTHER TINNED FISH

Ortiz
conservasortiz.com

Wild Planet
wildplanetfoods.com

CHILE CRISP

Fly by Jing
flybyjing.com

CRÈME FRAÎCHE AND OTHER DAIRY PRODUCTS

Bellwether Farms
bellwetherfarms.com

GOCHUJANG

Mother-in-Law's
milkimchi.com

Rhei-Maid
rheimaid.com

GOMASIO

Eden
edenfoods.com

Landsea Gomasio
brookebudner.squarespace.com/
    landsea-gomasio

HONEY

Zach & Zoë Sweet Bee Farm
zachandzoe.co

NOODLES, RICE, OTHER GRAINS, AND LEGUMES

Anson Mills
ansonmills.com

Central Milling
centralmilling.com

Koda Farms
kodafarms.com

Rancho Gordo
ranchogordo.com

Rancho Llano Seco
llanoseco.com

Rustichella d'Abruzzo
casarustichellain.com

Sfoglini
sfoglini.com

OLIVE OIL

California Olive Ranch
californiaoliveranch.com

Enzo Olive Oil
enzooliveoil.com

Exau
exauoliveoil.com

Pineapple Collaborative
pineapplecollaborative.com

Séka Hills
sekahills.com

SALT AND SPICES

Burlap & Barrel
burlapandbarrel.com

Diaspora Co.
diasporaco.com

Jacobsen Salt Co.
jacobsensalt.com

Kalustyan's
kalustyans.com

Maldon Spice Company
maldonsalt.co.uk

Oaktown Spice Shop
oaktownspiceshop.com

Penzeys Spices
penzeys.com

Zingerman's
zingermans.com

SESAME OIL

La Tourangelle
latourangelle.com

TAHINI

Soom
soomfoods.com

ACKNOWLEDGMENTS

I always read the acknowledgments of a book before I even glance at any other page. It's a habit I picked up from the days when I was dreaming of becoming a published author and I was eager and curious to learn more about the people behind books. While there's usually only one name on the cover, there are many others who help bring a book to life. Without their vital contributions, books wouldn't be as beautifully designed, edited, tested, typeset, or produced. I hope I can adequately convey my gratitude to the team of people who played a role in the creation of this cookbook.

Thank you to everyone at Artisan Books, especially publisher Lia Ronnen, whose knowledge and intuition is unparalleled. Thank you to editors Bella Lemos and Judy Pray; art director Suet Chong; production editor Carson Lombardi; copyeditor Mark McCauslin (how did I get so lucky to have you expertly copyedit my book?); the production team of Nancy Murray and Erica Huang; and publicist Theresa Collier.

Kitty Cowles, my dear friend and agent, your insight and brilliance made this book—and every book we've worked on together—better by leaps and bounds. I am still in awe that my name appears on the list of authors you represent.

Erin Scott, thank you for the gorgeous photographs and for your skill in prop styling. Neither of us could have imagined that we would be doing the photo shoot for this cookbook during a pandemic, and I will forever appreciate your flexibility, care, and drive to make it happen safely. Thanks also to the entire Scott family, particularly Lilah, for lending a hand and for letting me spend so much time in your garden and backyard. Thank you to kitchen assistant Bruce Cole for being on our quaran-team.

The recipes in this book were tested multiple times by a wonderful group affectionately known as the Testing Team. Thank you to Davita Urdang-Spencer, Gyu Park, Hannah Robie, Katie Kelley, Laura Bradley, Corinne Sengwe, Annie Zisk, Erika Lee, Jane Hausauer, Maïalène Wilkins, Celeste Saharig, Christina Billing, Courtney Cikach, Elise Carlton, Tim and Toni Carlton, Jessica Naecker, Emily Forscher, Taylor Schwartz, Amanda Sarley-Weng, Judith Mandel, Alissa Rimmon, Claire Bray, Ali Stieglitz, Edith Williams, Yoon Hur, Hollie Loson, Jessa Strayer, Alice Mount, Alyson Parkes, Lena Gebhard, Sonja Hernandez, Juliana Stone and Jared Stone, Rachel Hochstetler, Rena Kolhede, Alana Buckley, Erica Wrightson, Christine Binder, Dawn Nita, Natasha Bartolome and Ryan Hutson, Pinky Farnum, Tori Ambruso, Alexa Prendergast, Pam Pauley, Jocelyn Bradley, Dana Washington, Carly Haase-Duester, Allie Silvas, Maggie Bromberg, Natasha Nicolai, Paula Wade, Sofia Martin, Elizabeth Rothschild, Lisa Goldstein, Sophie Tivona, Jessica Plummer, Emery Sorvino, Wendy Lee and Nick Snead, Kathryn Phelan, Sarah Franklin, Paige Hermreck, Lauren Karas, Carly Dela Cruz, Victoria Stanell, Brittney Boehm, Hannah Davitian, Jess L'Esperance, Lisa Wahl, Sara Lopez-Isaacs, Jane Feinberg, Tom Purtill,

Sarah Fisher, Jaimi Boehm, Carly Hackbarth, Elizabeth Blanke, Clare Langan, Madeline Mihran, Rachial Parrish, Suzi Freitas, Taylor Lewis, Emily Burns, Coral Lee, Alex Lentz, Colleen Wahl, Stephanie Bohar, Emily Rusca, Julie Beigel-Coryell, Jen Nurse, Ashley Lasher, Sarah Cotey, Sydney Clark, Libby Bradley, and Kate Long.

Thank you to the hardworking farmers and producers who grow, pickle, ferment, cure, bottle, bake, or otherwise make the ingredients upon which these recipes rely. You are an endless source of inspiration. Thanks also to the booksellers who've championed *The Newlywed Table* and other books of mine. It has been such a pleasure to get to know you.

I'm grateful for the opportunities to collaborate with and learn from my heroes in the kitchen, most especially Suzanne Goin, Elisabeth Prueitt, Chad Robertson, Christina Tosi, Alice Waters, Yotam Ottolenghi, Fuchsia Dunlop, Nigel Slater, Nadiya Hussain, Yasmin Khan, Fabrizia Lanza, Deborah Madison, and Roxana Jullapat. You've taught me a great deal, and I often picture you all standing in my own little kitchen, cheering me on and offering advice.

To my family and friends, thank you so much for your love and support. I hope you know that I cherish you.

Graham Willis Bradley, you are the love of my life. Without you by my side, I would never have been able to write this cookbook. Thank you for encouraging me, believing in me, and always valuing my work. Cooking with you is my favorite thing to do. If we have one hundred more years together, it won't be enough.

INDEX

MARIA ZIZKA is a cookbook writer and recipe developer who was named by Forbes as one of the most influential people under thirty in the world of food and drink. She has coauthored numerous award-winning cookbooks, including *Tartine All Day, Everything I Want to Eat,* and *This Is Camino.* Her first solo cookbook, *The Newlywed Table,* was published in 2019. Zizka lives and cooks in the San Francisco Bay Area. Find her on Instagram at @mariazizka.